SMART CRYPTO

Legally Protect Your Hard Earned Wealth

Reclaiming Your Wealth & Identity

How Not to Pay Crypto Taxes (Legally) & Reclaim Your Birthright

by

Reverend Joseph Fain McDaniel

Disclaimer

Important Notice

This book and the materials herein are intended for educational and informational purposes only.

Nothing in this publication should be construed as legal, financial, or tax advice.

The examples, templates, and processes provided:

- Are based on historical, commercial, and administrative practices.
- Are intended to support private education and empowerment.
- Do not constitute the practice of law, banking, or financial services.

The authors and ministry assume no responsibility for any actions taken by readers based on the information presented.

All use is at the discretion and risk of the individual reader.

Readers are encouraged to:

- Conduct their own research,
- Consult appropriate private or professional counsel where needed,
- Act with honor, integrity, and full personal responsibility.

This publication is a private offering made under the auspices of a faith-based ministry, operating in the private domain, without intent to mislead, harm, or infringe upon the rights of others.

Thank you for respecting the spirit in which this work is offered: for education, empowerment, and peaceful private remedy.

Contents

Introduction

Let's get one thing straight this isn't some crypto-for-dummies guide. If you're here, you're ready to stop letting the system skim off your gains and start playing by your own rules. I've put in the work to uncover the legal paths to keep the government out of my crypto profits, and now I'm here to hand you the blueprint. This book? It's part guide, part manifesto, and all about breaking free from their fraudulent system.

Who Am I?

I'm not here to sell a dream or push hype. I'm a Minister on a mission to bring clarity where there's confusion. I've spent years working behind the scenes on major film and TV sets, translating complex digital setups into seamless movie magic. Studio heads call me when they need the impossible made simple—and that's been my gift: breaking down what stumps others and putting it in terms people actually understand.

I founded and successfully sold a web development and marketing company called TheMediaButler.com, where I still serve as a consultant. We've been the behind-the-scenes secret weapon for major influencers and companies—pulling the strings, making the magic happen quietly. That's where I honed my approach to life—less guru, more Dr. Strange outmaneuvering Thanos (minus the cape), or maybe just an ADHD mind wired for high-efficiency strategy.

But this book isn't about me. It's about giving you real, actionable steps to protect your crypto, reclaim your autonomy, and break free from the system's grip—with clarity, honor, and intention.

Part of my mission is to help others avoid the costly mistakes I made while building my company's and investments like crypto. The main goal of this book is to help YOU move smarter, faster, and confidently with peace.

Everything I've done before—every business, every venture—is just dust on my boots from running the rat race. The so-called "financial freedom" handed out by bosses and clients pales in comparison to what I'm about to share with you. This is the real deal: true freedom—spiritual, personal, and financial.

To join our private members community and be apart of our inner circle go apply at Title8.org

How This Guide Works

This isn't a promise of overnight freedom or a secret formula to beat the system. It's a collection of tools, ideas, and strategies I've explored and used myself. I'm not here to tell you what to do, just to offer what's worked for me in case it helps you build your own path. If you've got a vision and want more options outside the usual routes, this guide might give you a few pieces to work with.

Disclaimer

No BS here—I'm a private attorney-in-fact, not "at law," meaning I DO NOT hold a BAR card, nor am I a CPA or tax advisor. This book, along with the paired YouTube video, is provided purely for informational and educational purposes. What you choose to do with this information is entirely up to you. If you need professional advice, I encourage you to seek it—preferably from someone with the credentials to back it up, like Dr. Don Kilam, who holds multiple doctorates and expertise in these areas. So with out further hachoo let's get into it..

Chapter 1

The Crypto Conundrum

So, you've made some money in crypto real digital boss stuff. But the second you cash out to buy that house, there's a lineup of hands waiting to take a cut: the exchange, the IRS, your bank, your family, and friends! That's the lack system working against you. If you're tired of it, you're in the right place. This chapter is about comprehending why the general public's understanding of the "rules" in crypto aren't designed to benefit you and how you can legally sidestep them.

Rules or Misconception?

Following the standard system with crypto means facing capital gains taxes, KYC (Know Your Customer) rules, and transaction fees at every turn. Meanwhile, the big players get their share, leaving you with the scraps.

Here's the truth: regulations are there to keep your profits under control. You could follow every rule, fill out every form, and pay every tax but at the end of the day, you'll see just how much they take. That's why this book exists: to show you how to keep what's yours. The wealthy private crypto pro's aren't playing by the same rules you are. Neither are the crypto exchanges for that matter! Ever wondered why when you buy from crypto.com your bank charges international fees? I'll answer why…

Why Going by the Book Isn't Always "Fair"

Let's break it down. You work hard, you get paid for working hard, but before that paycheck even hits your account, it's taxed to oblivion. Then, you decide to invest some of those post-tax earnings maybe in stocks, real estate, rare motorcycles, Beanie Babies, or crypto. If you see any profit on your hard-earned, already-taxed money, they swoop in again for another slice in capital gains tax. That's right money you already paid taxes on gets taxed again just for growing.

And it doesn't stop there. Buy something? Here comes sales tax, piling on top of income tax, nibbling away at the same dollar every time it moves. Want to gift a car you've already paid taxes on to a friend or family member? They get hit with taxes too—just for accepting something that you, and probably 100 other people, already paid taxes on!

Now imagine making a 40% profit on an investment—money that's technically yours. But to the IRS, it's as if they're entitled to it, no matter how much you've already paid. And now? They're even talking about taxing unrealized gains—money you haven't even cashed out yet. Insane, right? It feels like a tactic to keep you from making any moves they can't control.

Does this sound like a reward for your hard work? You're not alone in feeling fed up. This isn't about avoiding responsibility; it's about breaking the endless cycle of losing your hard-earned money just because it moves from one hand to another.

The Alternative: Become A Foreigner

"I know—that's probably what you're thinking right now. "Ok.. sure like I have time to go through that mess..." or "This sounds too good to be true... or dangerous... and could get me in trouble."

Relax. Karen, you need a spanking for that fear-based mindset. We're not doing anything illegal here—we're just playing the same game they are... but better. NO this isn't some stupid sovereign citizen "*Go to my YouTube channel*" rabbit hole I promise this ain't that. I still pay for Netflix.

If you want to keep more of your profits, it's time to start looking outside the U.S. There are countries and digital residency programs that don't come with the same restrictions. It's A LOT easier than you think! Take the Palau Digital Residency, for example—you're legally recognized outside U.S. jurisdiction. This means:

- You can use crypto exchanges that don't restrict your transactions.
- You avoid unnecessary taxes and high fees*
- You can operate legally and keep your profits knowing how to move correctly

My Story: The Journey to Crypto Freedom

So here's how this whole thing started: I got into crypto like most people, hoping to turn a profit and enjoy the freedom it promised. But once I actually made money, I realized that cashing out wasn't as straightforward as I'd hoped. The moment I wanted to convert some of my gains, it was like a spotlight turned on—suddenly, every bank, exchange, and tax agency wanted a cut.

At first, I thought I was missing something. I mean, isn't the whole point of crypto to be free from that stuff? But it turns out, if you're a U.S. citizen, freedom isn't as free as it sounds. Even the decentralized nature of crypto doesn't fully protect you if you're playing in the U.S. system; or any commercial law system the Kingship government still wants their share of every trade, cashout, and transaction. I felt like I was right back in the system I thought I'd escaped, and I wasn't about to accept that.

So What Would The Smart Ultra Rich Do?

I started digging. If the standard route meant endless taxes and fees, then I needed to find a new path. It's funny—when you start looking outside the usual routes, you realize just how many people out there are also searching for ways to legally avoid unnecessary oversight.

That's when I found out about the Palau Digital Residency program. At first, it sounded too good to be true. A Palau government-issued ID that allows me to pass KYC and doesn't come with the typical U.S. strings attached? And I can get it processed in a few weeks for only $250 bucks! What?! The more I researched and looked into other big player doing the same, the more it clicked it's a legitimate, legal solution, and exactly what I'd been looking for.

Palau Down and Plow Through the Barriers! Your Gateway to Privacy and Diplomatic Freedom

Getting set up with Palau was a turning point for me. I realized that I didn't need to be a citizen of the U.S. in the way they'd defined it. With Palau's Digital Residency, I could get a legal ID and foreign status! All while staying right where I was. And the best part? It didn't cost a fortune—just a couple hundred bucks and a little patience.

Obtaining the Palau ID was the critical part of the equation. Unfortunately, most exchanges still assume your nationality based on your IP address. So, I set up a VPN to keep my location private, reflect my "international" status/citizenship with my IP, and make sure my transactions could move freely. What's the best way to do this? I'll save you the trial-and-error: NordVPN is hands-down the fastest, easiest, and best I've used. Use this discount link and you'll get three free months: https://refer-nordvpn.com/psHKPguGmzH.

With the Palau residency and a VPN, I was finally able to access exchanges with way lower fees than anything you'll find on U.S. platforms. It was like lifting a weight off—no more getting gouged at every step. Now, I was finally experiencing the freedom crypto promised, and it actually felt real.

So that's how I ended up here, laying out everything I've learned. This isn't a guide from an "expert"; it's just a blueprint from someone who's done the research, made the mistakes, and figured out a way to keep more of what's mine.

Now that you know where this is all coming from, let's dive into the first steps of obtaining your Palau residency.

Chapter 2

Setting Up Your Palau Digital Residency

Getting the Palau Digital Residency is a game-changer. This residency offers you a legit way to gain access to exchanges and other financial services that usually lock out U.S. users out. Plus, it's affordable and requires zero relocation.

This chapter will break down exactly how to apply, why it works, and the step-by-step you'll need to get set up. Let's dig in.

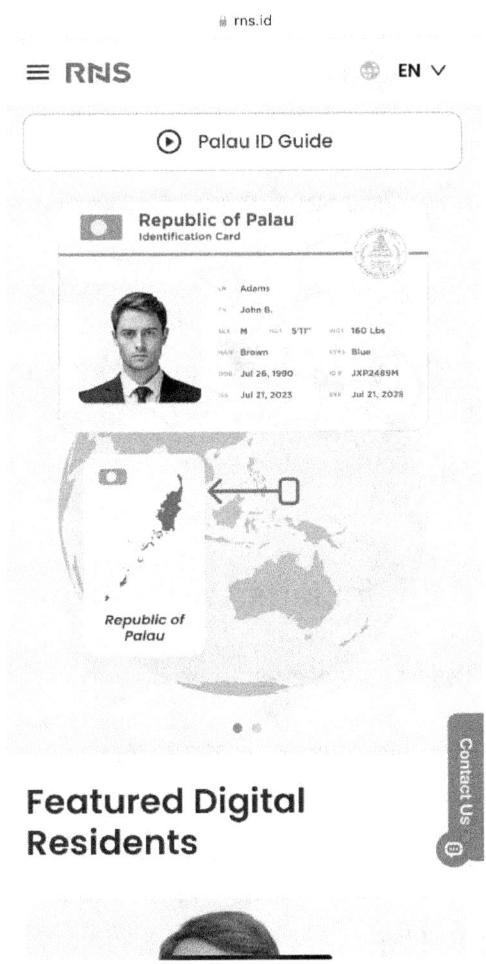

Why the Palau Residency Matters

Palau's Digital Residency Program isn't citizenship, but it gives you a recognized ID and residency without the strings attached. You can use it for:

- Global Access to Exchanges: With your residency ID, you'll have access to exchanges that block U.S. citizens.
- Lower Fees: These international platforms often have better fee structures.
- Legal Recognition Outside the U.S. You're recognized as a resident of Palau, giving you freedom from U.S.-specific regulations in certain cases.
- Gets you foreign national status (lots of perks if you know how to use it right)

Additionally, the Palau ID functions similarly to a driver's license or state ID, allowing you to perform various identification tasks. It's also possible to obtain a Palauan driver's license, which may offer different legal considerations regarding traffic stops and regulations.

Getting Started with the Application

Let's go step-by-step on how to set this up:

1. Start the Application: Head to the official Palau residency site. They'll ask for basic info, a passport photo, and your actual passport or ID. No social security number needed. If you want some extra karma points, use my referral link: https://rns.id/?rc_by=OhxlPfjq.

2. Choose Your Plan: Plans vary by length (one year, five years, etc.), with costs starting around $250.

3. Approval Process: After submission, it takes about three to four weeks to get approved. You'll receive your Palau government verified ID.

Putting It All Together

Once you have the Palau ID and VPN set up:

- With your Palau ID, these exchanges will pass you through KYC without U.S. restrictions.
- Access low fee Exchanges: Sign up on international exchanges like OKX, Bitget, BingX, kraken, and possibly Binance. Some people have reported trouble passing Binance KYC.
- Enjoy Lower Fees: With the right exchange, you'll be trading with better fee structures and keeping more of what's yours.
- Stay Private: Use your VPN consistently to avoid unnecessary tracking or account issues. The goal is to stay off the radar and operate freely.

Now your all KY lubed up sliding through the Check with the Palau ID! How's it feel? Now that you know how to leverage digital residency, let's add another layer of protection—by turning your name into a real asset!

All of this was great but I still had a problem… something festering in the back of my mind. Have you ever felt, deep down in your spirit and soul that something isn't right? Like the system is all **BS**? Like your "money" and property is really just IOU's you can never fully own? You might be on to something!

Chapter 3

The Turning Point – Meeting Don Kilam

So here I was, thinking I'd finally cracked the code with my Palau ID and VPN setup. I could access exchanges, lower transaction fees, and explore platforms with fewer restrictions for U.S. citizens. But there was still one big challenge—the crypto I'd previously bought and traded through accounts connected to my Social Security number remained within the scope of IRS reporting. Any future transactions could still be subject to scrutiny, bringing with them potential tax implications, audits, and government takes.

It felt like I'd just managed to step outside one cage and into another. Then, right around this time, I came across a guy who sparked my third eye like Buddha's tax-savvy cousin or some rogue CPA with a knack for talking in mysterious legal source code. This was Dr. Don Kilam—a man who seemed like a blend of Tony Soprano and a Zen monk if that monk had two doctorates in law, and a permanent gold and diamond encrusted grill.

Following a Higher Authority: Embracing Natural Law Over Coercion and Fraud

Don Kilam's teachings hit me like a freight train. According to him, what most of us think of as "the law" is actually a cleverly designed system of coercion and legal tricks that makes us sign away our rights. We aren't the ones bending the rules here—they are. The government uses a slick setup of forms and agreements to claim fiduciary control of our assets and estate. Turning you into a "infant or incompetent someone of unsound mind". They run the psyche ward and your their pacient. At least until you say otherwise.

The ALL CAPS NAME isn't actually "you" at all. It's a **Cestui Que Vie Trust** or Sole Proprietorship—a non-living entity or "corporate legal fiction" created by the government after birth when your mother signed you over as "informant" as shown on the birth certificate. She informed the state their was property and registered it. When you were recorded and registered with **vital statistics and records.** The word "regis," meaning to give up ownership to the "king" or authority, reveals the essence of this system.

Your **Social Security Number** serves as the registration number for this property, or "bill of lading" recorded in the vital records of the District of Columbia—or, in simpler terms, the **United States Corporation** not to be confused with the land and soil known as **"The United States of America" as stated in the constitution.** One exists in the sea the other exists on land... but we'll get to that later.

Food for thought—record companies claim ownership over your essence, likeness, and vibration or in other words your sound. Ever heard the phrase **"selling your soul for a record deal"?** They're not being metaphorical. By their logic, "you" are a product, they're your creators, and they own you. First rule in law is: YOU DONT CONTROL ANYTHING YOU DONT CREATE.

Marinate on that for a minute.

They've tricked us into treating this legal non living entity as our identity. A dead mindless consumer In reality, there's a distinct split: the **natural-born person** and the **legal entity.** The system takes advantage of this by making you believe the two are one and the same, but they're not. Even worse, they legally declare you **"incompetent, not of sound mind to self-govern,"** which gives them authority over you.

Once you **overstand** this, you can begin to reclaim what's yours.

Becoming the Trustee and Beneficiary of Your Own Life

One of the most game-changing revaluations was the power of something called "status correction" involving taking control of that ALL CAPS NAME and making "the system" better work for you. By correcting your status on the land and soil, ending the estoppel with the IRS, making your ALL CAPS NAME a business (LLC) within a holding company, and trust.. You can start to move like the ultra-wealthy! The ultra-wealthy know their birthright, they know who they are and they claim it! Trump said in debate vs Hillary *"Knowing the tax code makes me smart not a criminal. You and your friends use the same tax laws I do…"* that quote isn't meant to be political btw so calm down all you Trump lovers & haters.

In this setup, you're no longer just a taxpayer—you revert back to your natural status as a U.S. National, foreign to the United States corporation, just as Palau or France would be. Foreign. You're operating under natural law and common law. Not under corporate statutes. Your at peace with the system, but not owned or controlled by it. No longer a 14th Amendment citizen, no longer property—just a free, living man or woman with rights intact and jurisdiction free and clear.

This isn't about evasion or rebellion—it's about correction. A lawful return to your rightful status and standing. Not fiction. Not theory. Just the truth hidden in plain sight. When your affairs are structured correctly, and your position is clearly stated, you can finally operate with the protections and freedom intended by both divine and constitutional law.

It's Not You... It's Just Your Monster

Every official document uses the all-caps version of your name—what some call the "strawman," sole proprietor, or legal fiction. You confuse this entity with the real you, and by doing so, you're considered "of unsound mind" or legally an "infant"—someone not capable of managing or governing their own affairs. After all, your word is your bond. And if you're saying obviously untrue things—like telling a judge you're a non-living legal entity (a "dead thing") while standing in front of him breathing and talking—he's going to conclude you're not of sound mind and therefore subject to his governance. Legally, that makes you an idiot. And when that happens, they'll happily govern for you—and pay themselves very well to do it.

LET ME SAY THIS VERY CLEARLY ITS NOT HARD TO CORRECT STATUS! Only hard thing is unlearning the bad generational programming around how money works. Some people out there still believe the dollar is backed by gold held Fort Knox. I was recently told this by a bank teller of all people 🤦 That's why I'm writing this book. We have to educate these young people shit is getting out of hand! STOP GROVELING FOR PENNIES ITS YOUR CREDIT NOT THEIRS!

GO JG Wentworth on their ass! "it's YOUR money use it NOW!" otherwise wait till 65, get less than pennies of what they actually owe you, and let that death benefit go to them instead of your family. Just like how Walmart does on their employees. I digress.

By correcting your status and reclaiming the entity they use as a debt-slave, you step outside their corporate circle—jerkistiction—and their rules. This strategy not only grants you privacy but also helps protect you from probate courts, excessive taxation, and claims on your property.

And hey it's probably time to get out of those murky waters of admiralty anyway… those butt-buddy banker pirates are a little too comfortable getting up in your "business" if you know what I mean. All jokes aside let's get to the nitty gritty.

The New Game Plan

With the help of Don's teachings, I finally saw the way to make my setup untouchable. With the combination of trademark protections, trusts, foreign status, and the Palau ID I would have everything I needed to make sure my crypto gains, assets, and legacy were protected.

Most people hear "trust" and picture a billionaire's tax shelter or that vague "thing" their lawyer mentioned before handing them a massive bill. That misconception keeps lawyers' wine fridges stocked. So yeah, if you're going for that kind of trust, you probably do need to be rich—just to cover the fees. But this? This isn't that. This is about reclaiming control, not funding a lawyer's next vacation. Now that you've got digital residency, let's take it up a notch and turn your name into a real, untouchable asset.

Chapter 4

Status Correction – Breaking Free from the System

If you're serious about learning how to navigate the system and stop volunteering your labor and hard-earned money then the first thing you need to understand is status correction. Getting back on the land and soil of the actual republic of the codified states. As stated in the pledge of allegiance: "I pledge allegiance to the flag of the United States of America AND the Republic for which it stands" TWO SEPARATE ENTITIES! Did you ever catch that before?

Yes the assembly of states still exists till this day and they will help you status correct. Please remember this isn't just about filling out forms—it's about understanding how your legal identity shapes your interaction with the system. The way you're classified determines whether you're seen as a taxpayer, a federal citizen, or something entirely different.

The problem is, most of us unknowingly volunteer for federal citizenship, a status that comes with obligations we never consciously agreed to. To truly use the system to your advantage, you need to understand its roots: the 14th Amendment, the banking crisis, and the way federal citizenship was engineered.

The 14th Amendment: A Tool for Usurpation

When the 14th Amendment was (sort of) passed, it introduced a new type of "citizen"—the federal citizen. Initially, this status was designed for freed slaves, granting them "privileges"under the federal government. But it didn't take long for this classification to extend to all Americans, effectively placing everyone under federal jurisdiction.

Here's the kicker: the 14th Amendment was never ratified by all the states, which means its legitimacy is, at best, questionable. Despite this shaky foundation, it's been weaponized as one of the most powerful tools of control over the American people. Even Congress has called it the "greatest tool for usurpation on the American people."

This amendment became the legal backbone for everything from taxes and fines to censorship, policing, and ultimate control over our lives. It's why we're forced to pay to be policed, fined, governed, and managed. And while they say participation is voluntary, it's often enforced through coercion, intimidation, and outright fraud.

A crucial piece of this history involves President Lincoln's vision for equality. He supported equal rights, but not the creation of a new class of federally controlled citizenship. Some researchers and legal theorists believe this opposition to centralized power was one of the deeper reasons behind his assassination. His vision emphasized unity and equality without expanding federal control—a vision many argue the 14th Amendment reversed by redefining citizenship and tying individuals directly to federal corporate maritime or "admiralty" jurisdiction.

If you're interested in digging deeper into this history, the *Slaughterhouse Cases* are a great study. These landmark Supreme

Court cases dissected the distinctions between state and federal citizenship, shedding light on the profound implications of the 14th Amendment. It's a valuable starting point for understanding how this system evolved into what we know today.

Redefining the Definition of the Term "Person"

The 14th Amendment didn't just create federal citizenship; it also redefined the word "person" to include trusts, corporations, partnerships, associations, joint-stock companies, unincorporated organizations, and even governments. So, when you see "State of California vs. John Doe," it's because the state, legally speaking, is also considered a "person."

This change allows the government to treat states, corporations, and individuals as equal "persons" under the law, creating a system where non-living entities can have the same legal rights and responsibilities as actual people. The reality? These entities are non-living creatures of law. For an absurd example, you could put your cat in a trust, and it would have the legal rights of a person. Yes, people have actually done this.

The Banking Crisis: We Became the Collateral

In 1933, the U.S. went off the gold standard, shifting the dollar from being backed by gold and silver coins to being backed by our labor—or, more specifically, the "full faith and credit of the FUTURE LABOR of the American Citizen." Yes, we became the collateral for the currency, turning each citizen into credit and forced to use debt instruments owned by a "federal reserve" that's not federal and holds no reserves!

Its almost comical if it wasn't so tragically true. Let me say this again "dollars" are IOU's backed by our future labor = credit.

The Federal Reserve NOTES, as they're often called. Promissory notes—or what most people think of as "dollars". Technically, a dollar is defined as 371.25 grains of pure silver (approximately 24.057 grams). If you want to dig deeper into that, check out the Coinage Act of 1792. Spoiler alert we were never meant to be on fiat currency. This departure from the founding documents of America voided everything we fought for in the revolutionary war. As famously stated by Thomas Jefferson.

This banking crisis system relies on a perpetual state of "war and crisis" to stay afloat. Every dollar in circulation isn't wealth—it's debt, backed by the future work and earnings of U.S. citizens. We're not just taxpayers; we're the principal investors in an endless debt scheme. This is why every president since 1933 has had a war. If you've served in the military, you were told we're always in a state of war. It's not just rhetoric—it's a legal basis and a necessity for this giant PONZI scheme to function.

BUT here's the upside: if it's all IOUs, and your the principal investor then legally and lawfully it's your credit! Your money! They just have fiduciary control which requires them to act honorably. They are supposed to be working for you! Naughty little contractors. Time to make they pay up and watch them squirm!

Correcting Your Status: The Path to True Independence

Status correction is about removing yourself from the classification of "federal citizen" and reclaiming a nationality that isn't tied to the corporate U.S. For example, I don't identify as a federal citizen. I domicile in the Kingdom of Hawaii, making me a Hawaiian national or a Palauian. If you're in California, you could choose to be a national of the Republic of California, reclaiming your identity within a different jurisdiction. This makes you foreign to the District of Columbia. This shift has a real impact on your your whole legal standing, including tax liability and other obligations.

Correcting your status involves getting back on the land and soil, acting as the living man. Not a corporate entity or taxpayer. This is easily done. You can make your own documents or order a done for you packet from MyStatusSelect.com they will put you in touch with your state assembly recorder and get your status corrected on the record with the Land Recording Office. This is how you officially "opt-out" of their supposedly "voluntary tax aystem" this also requires filing a few forms with the IRS to put them on notice of the change in status. Lots of information online about this. Moving on to the next super secret sauce move.. Turning your name into a business!

Your Name as a Business: Taking Control of the All-Caps Name

Remember that ALL CAPS NAME they use on official documents? That's not actually "you." It's a corporate entity, representing a trust. First rule in law: You can't control what you didn't create. So if you want to take ownership of your identity, follow what I call the Michael Jordan method—turn your name into a licensed, trademarked business.

Celebrities and politicians do this all the time. They turn that ALL CAPS name into an LLC, often filed in a state like Wyoming, Nevada, or Delaware—places known for strong charging order protections. This not only gives your more privacy but also gives you fiduciary (trustee/executor) control over the legal entity tied to your name.

Here's the catch: the system treats you as if you're legally incompetent—like an infant or someone of unsound mind—unfit to manage your own affairs. And since they never explained this to you, they assume the role of trustee and handle it for you... while paying themselves very, very well.

Taking this step is how you start managing what was always meant to be.

I recommend using Northwest Registered Agents to set up your LLC. Thats who I personally use. They have the best prices and customer support. Click the link above I got you guys a major discounts

Chapter 5

Trademarking Your Name – Owning Your Identity

Now that you've set up your LLC and corrected your status, the next step is to take full control over your name by trademarking it. This isn't just a legal technicality—it's about making sure no one, not the government, not some sneaky corporation, can mess with or profit off your name. Think of this step as locking the front door to your identity. Your ALL CAPS NAME has been used against you for far too long. It's time to take it back.

Why Trademarking Your Name Matters

Here's the deal: your ALL CAPS NAME—the one that shows up on every official document—was created at birth as a separate legal entity. Yeah, it's not really you, but they've been treating it that way to claim control. Trademarking your name is about flipping the script. Once you trademark it, you're making it crystal clear: This name? It's mine. Hands off. Trademarking doesn't just stop others from using your name; it transforms it into a powerful asset.

Trying to use my name on a bill? Better pay the owner first—because that name is a registered trademark of Sound & Stone Records Trust. Otherwise, damages will be sought—simple as that. And yes, this applies to court cases too. Remember, the judge is calling that ALL CAPS NAME, not you. Some judges don't even realize this themselves—they're just following tradition and programming. But real, high-level judges do know. The average lawyer or fake judge they toss into traffic court? Yeah… not so much.

Setting Up Your LLC (Without Using Your Social)

Here's where it gets fun: When you set up your LLC, you don't have to link it to your Social Security Number. Why? Because your social is how they keep the game rigged. By separating your ALL CAPS NAME (the business entity) from yourself (the living, breathing you), you create a firewall.

How do you do this? There are alternative routes to getting an EIN (Employer Identification Number) that don't require your SSN. It keeps everything clean, separate, and under your control. For more details, check out the the Title 8 ministry. They help people fill out the SS4 form needed to obtain an EIN numbers without needing a social. Check them out at Title8.org

The Steps to Trademarking Your Name

Trademarking and copyrighting your name is a game-changer. It's not just about blocking others from using it—it's about taking your name and turning it into an iron-clad legal weapon.

Here's the 411:

1. Know What They've Been Doing Behind Your Back.

Let's start with some truth bombs:

- Your name has been treated as a negotiable instrument, tied directly to your labor and your trust. Yes—it's your credit they're using… and they're making you pay it back with interest.
- Under 42 USC § 408 and UCC 3-104, your identity is leveraged as collateral. They create debt instruments using your name, then sell you—the legal fiction—on secondary markets, without your knowledge or consent. That's securitization without disclosure—and that's illegal.
- But here's where it gets better: when you trademark your name, it's game over. Now, if they continue to use it, you've got them not just on security fraud, but trademark infringement too. If they mess with your estate "straight to jail!"

By correcting your status, you're no longer a ward of the state. By trademarking your all caps name they can't just treat your identity like free collateral anymore. And if they try? You have standing to hold them accountable—legally and lawfully. Put some respect on your name.

After all… you are royalty.

2. Apply for a Trademark:

Once your name is secured, it's time to trademark it through the USPTO (United States Patent and Trademark Office). This gives you exclusive rights to your name, meaning no one can profit off it or use it without your permission.

3. File a UCC-1 Financing Statement:

This is where the real fun begins. Filing a UCC-1 statement makes your name legally yours. It creates a secured interest in your name and establishes a claim that no one else can touch. Best to do this from a holding company or trust NOT your personal name or business.

4. Flex Your Rights:

Trademarking isn't just paperwork; it's power. If someone tries to use your name—whether it's a company, a scammer, or even the government—you have the legal ammunition to shut them down.

The Media Butler offers a offer a done for you trademarking service that will trademark your brand, all caps name, thumbprint. and signature. All the things they use to steal your credit. To be blunt and honest the application and approval process sucks. Its is a lot of work and the USPTO website is terrible! Save yourself the time, money, and headache I endured trying to figure it out myself and hire an expert like TheMediaButler.com.

Chapter 6

"Donald Trump, Warren Buffett, & 'I' Walk Into a Trust..."

This is it—the strategy that separates the truly free from those trapped in the system's web: "own nothing, control everything." This ultimate move isn't just for the rich and powerful; it's for anyone ready to take control of their life and legacy. The concept is simple yet transformative: Relinquish official ownership of assets while retaining full control through trusts and other legal structures. By doing so, you shield your wealth from heavy tax burdens, lawsuits, and liabilities, operating with greater autonomy. It's a strategy that's been quietly embraced by some of the wealthiest and most influential figures in history.

The Legal Proof: You're Funding the System

Your worth a lot of money! The United States of America is a business! It has a DUNS number. What's it's product or service you ask? The Citizen. Still skeptical? Look up 15 USC § 4724(e)(1) Definition: "United States Business means: United states Citizen" so there your have it. This is why they go to war for you.

United States business

(1) the term "United States business" means— (A) a United States citizen; (B) a corporation, partnership, or other association created under the laws of the United States or of any State (including the District of Columbia or any commonwealth, territory, or possession of the United States); or (C) a foreign corporation, partnership, or other association, more than 95 percent of which is owned by persons described in subparagraphs (A) and (B); and

Source
15 USC § 4724(e)(1)

Scoping language
As used in this section

Is this correct? okay or

Proof that the Cestui Que Vie Act is part of the USC 👀

Cornell Law School

Search Cornell

LII Legal Information Institute

Menu

38 U.S. Code § 108 - Seven-year absence presumption of death

Your Labor = The Collateral

According to *31 USC 5118*, the dollar isn't backed by gold or silver—it's backed by the "full faith and credit of the American people." In plain terms, your labor, assets, and future earnings are the collateral holding up the entire monetary system.

Your Signature = Their Loan

Under *12 USC 1431* and *15 USC 1602(g)*, your signature on financial agreements creates the value behind transactions. Banks don't lend you their money—they monetize your signature and use it to fund the loan. In essence, you're financing your own debt.

The Social Security Trap

Per *42 USC 408*, your Social Security number isn't just an ID—it's the key to the system. This number links you to the ALL CAPS NAME, the legal fiction that turns you into collateral and locks you into their economic game without knowing the rules.

Negotiable Instruments = Their Hidden Playbook

Laws like *UCC 3-104* classify promissory notes, checks, and agreements as negotiable instruments. These documents carry value because of your signature, and the system profits from them while treating you as the debtor.

By understanding these laws, it becomes clear why the "own nothing, control everything" strategy is so effective. Filing a UCC-1 Financing Statement and creating trusts isn't about exploiting loopholes—it's about reclaiming your position and shielding your assets. We act in honor. They are the ones in dishonor using coercion and obfuscating the truth for their own financial gain.

The Trust Strategy – In Brief

At the core of this strategy are trusts—powerful tools that allow you to hold and manage assets without officially owning them. This shields those assets from liabilities, taxes, and judgments. The old "own nothing, control everything" trick. But let's be clear: we're not talking about cookie-cutter trusts set up by shady BAR-card lawyers.

Sidebar: What's a BAR Card?

A BAR card isn't a license; it's a membership under the *British Accreditation Registry (BAR)*. Lawyers serve two masters: the BAR association and their clients. How can they truly serve you when they're subservient to a foreign authority operating as a business? Let's not forget that court is also a business; the judge literally sits on a *BANC* (a term derived from "bank") because they profit off your estate.

Matthew 6:24 (KJV):

"No man can serve two masters: for either he will hate the one, and love the other; or else he will hold to the one, and despise the other. Ye cannot serve God and mammon."

Instead, we're talking about private trusts one for example: the **non-grantor irrevocable complex discretionary spendthrift trusts** and my personal favorite a **508(c)(1)(A) Ministry Trust.** These structures offer maximum protection and control, shielding assets while giving you full authority over them. I highly recommend The Intelligent Banker's book "The Trust Codex" To learn more about these types of trusts, check out the resources offered by Title 8 Ministry, which not only provides training materials but also helps individuals create trusts like this themselves. Josh, the author of The Intelligent Banker, charges around $28,000 to set one up—so if you're balling on a budget, it's worth reaching out to the ministry and learning how to do it yourself.

Real-World Examples of "Own Nothing, Control Everything"

This isn't just theory; some of the wealthiest and most influential people have perfected this model:

- **Warren Buffett**: Famously quoted as saying he pays less in taxes than his secretary. Why? Because he structures his wealth to minimize tax liability, with trusts being a key part of that strategy.
- **The Kennedy Family**: When a tragic accident involving a Kennedy led to a lawsuit, their trust structure protected the family wealth. By not officially "owning" their assets, they shielded their fortune from legal claims—without paying a single cent.
- **Donald Trump**: Trump's companies have faced multiple bankruptcies without impacting his personal wealth. He owns nothing outright; instead, he manages assets through various entities and trusts, keeping his personal holdings untouchable.

These examples illustrate how trusts can be strategically designed to maintain complete control over assets while shielding them from taxes and liabilities.

Real-World Applications of "Own Nothing, Control Everything"

This strategy isn't just theoretical—it's been effectively used by some of the wealthiest individuals to protect their fortunes and avoid liabilities. By structuring their assets to be untouchable, they retain full control without the risks of direct ownership.

The best part? These principles aren't reserved for billionaires. They can be applied to anyone's life, regardless of financial status. The key is understanding how to leverage trusts and other legal tools to create a protective barrier around your wealth.

Putting It All Together

By combining **status correction**, making your name a business, trademarking your name, and establishing a trust structure, you're building a legal fortress around your assets.

The ultimate goal is simple: own nothing, control everything. When you officially "own" nothing, you minimize liabilities, tax obligations, and exposure to legal claims. Yet, through trusts and other structures, you retain full control and authority over your wealth.

Pro Tip:

If you're looking to fund your trust with real, tangible assets, start with precious metals—gold, silver, numismatic graded coins, legal tender silver certificates, and collectibles. For the absolute best deals on precious metals, I highly recommend Coins Plus. They're a wholesale dealer known for their ethical practices, speed, and professionalism. I used to work there, so trust me—they're the real deal. If you give them a call, ask for Ericka and be sure to mention my name (Joe) for a friendly connection and possibly an even better deal. 😉

Chapter 7

Stepping Out of Babylon

You've made it this far; you're seeing beyond the surface. The system we've uncovered isn't just a legal trap—it's a life trap. But here's the truth: you don't have to stay in it.

Recognizing System for What It Is

When the Court "seeks a judgment" and finds you in dishonor or default this allows the system to create bonds, securities, and debts in your name—bought and sold on the secondary market without your knowledge or consent. Why? Because money is credit—a promise backed by your future labor. But now, they've twisted it so you're paying it off twice! Not just with that future labor, but with the money you've already earned from it (of which was also taxed). Dipping deep into the pockets of your free will, stealing your "full faith and credit"—a phrase that really means your future energy, time, and worth.

Consider this: the judge in a courtroom wears black robes of mourning, representing himself as a "father" presiding over the "dead." Why mourning? Because when you show up as the ALL CAPS NAME—a non-living, dead entity—you're seen as incompetent to manage your life or estate.

Now compare that to the Pope, wearing white robes, symbolizing the "born again" soul. This twisted impersonation of our Heavenly Father claims to offer redemption from the very systems they created. It's a counterfeit authority designed to pull you away from your Creator. And all the while, they ask you to put your "trust" in their institutions.

But "In God We Trust" holds a meaning far deeper than their financial motives. It's a reminder that our allegiance, true citizenship, and trust belong to the Creator alone.

For more on how the prison bonds prop up the financial system read: "Word Is Bond - Don Kilam" this gets deep into the intricates.

A Direct Command

Verses that stands out:

"Come out of Babylon, my people, so that you do not participate in her sins and suffer from any of her plagues" - Revelation 18:4

"My people are destroyed for lack of knowledge: because thou hast rejected knowledge, I will also reject thee, that thou shalt be no priest to me: seeing thou hast forgotten the law of thy God, I will also forget thy children." - Hosea 4:6 (KJV):

Ignorance of the law is no excuse—not in court, not in contracts, and certainly not in life. Just because you didn't know doesn't mean they won't hold you accountable.

This isn't metaphorical; it's a direct command. In this sense Babylon represents the structures and systems designed to control us by making us believe we're bound to them. The ALL CAPS NAME—the “dead” legal entity—is the very definition of being “of the world.” But you are not dead—you’re a living, breathing Man endowed by the Creator with certain unalienable Rights, that among these are Life, Liberty, and the pursuit of Happiness!

Did you know the Bible is considered a LEGAL FACT in the courtroom! That should tell you something. It’s of the highes jurisdiction even above the judge. People have won court cases quoting only Bible verses that support their stance.

When you grasp this trickery and see the systems at play, the Bible takes on a new light. Its deeper meanings unlock, and suddenly, you see how much of what the system demands contradicts God’s command for us to be free. The rules, contracts, and coercion—they all stand against His word to live free under God, not man-made systems.

Faith without works is dead. Living without understanding is just as limiting. “Confusion comes from the devil; clarity comes from God.” So who are you in line with? Prayer and meditation are powerful tools—use them. It’s time to learn, take action, and step out of these systems in every way possible.

The Power of Unity

When you start this journey, especially with family, you create a shared purpose that’s powerful beyond measure.

In law, many cases require “two or more” witnesses for validity. The Bible, and other religious and esoteric texts, speak of the power in “where two or more are gathered.” Studies show that when two or more—especially family—learn together, retention, comprehension, and action grow exponentially.

Iron sharpens iron. Working together, each person's strengths elevate the others, forming an unstoppable force.

No family? Make your own tribe! I'm looking for smart, motivated people who are serious about bettering themselves daily—in this and in life in general. Be part of my tribe. Let's grow, learn, and succeed together.

Don't Let Self-Doubt Stop You

Don't let fear or self-doubt hold you back. If you can read, you can learn this. You don't need a law degree or a government title to understand and take back what's yours. Small steps add up, and the journey itself will teach you. With every bit of knowledge, another layer of deception falls away, and what remains is real freedom. This is the path out of Babylon, but you must first believe that you're capable of walking it.

Moving Forward

The concepts in this book are only the beginning. They're here to inspire you to dive deeper and take action. For those ready to go further, I highly recommend it! Lol I promise if you haven't already... YOU WILL FIND YOUR PURPOSE ON THIS PATH.

But remember: **knowledge without action is just theory.** Now is the time to move. Don't wait for the "perfect" moment or until you feel completely ready—that moment doesn't exist. Take one step today, then another tomorrow. Each step will build your confidence and deepen your understanding.

This is more than a book; it's a call to reclaim what's yours. It's about refusing to be "of the world" when you can stand independently.

Closing Thoughts

At the end of the day, remember: no matter what labels or documents the world imposes on you, you belong to a higher authority. You've been equipped with pure source power—it's up to you to tap into it.

True freedom starts with reclaiming who you are in your true power—not in the eyes of corporations or governments. This is your moment to choose life and live it abundantly—free from the constraints they've built around you.

As you move forward, may you find the clarity, courage, and strength to live fully and authentically, true to who you really are.

Prosperity is our Divine birthright. The game is clear now. You see it for what it is. The question is: **What are you going to do about it?**

"You shall know the truth and the truth shall set you free" - John 8:32

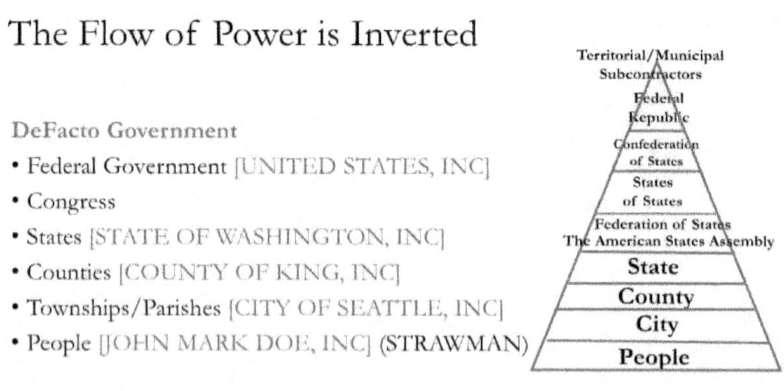

The Way Power is Supposed to Flow in America

DeJure Land Government

- People [John Mark Doe]
- Townships/Parishes [Seattle]
- Counties [King County]
- States [Washington State]
- Federation of States Assembly (Delegated)
- Confederation of States (Delegated)
- Federal Republic (Delegated)

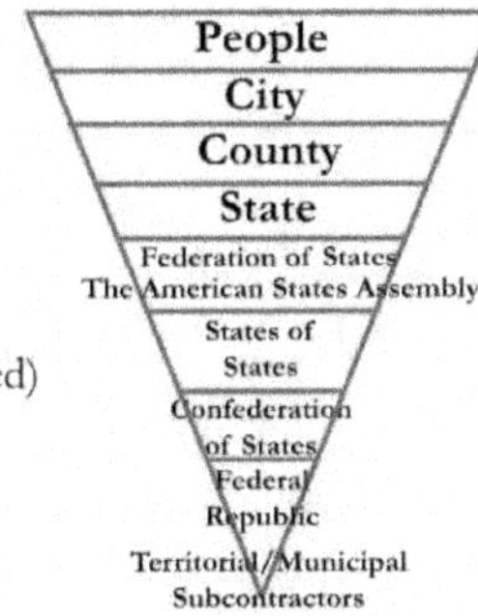

From DeFacto to DeJure. It's time, Neo. Follow the white rabbit.

Stay Connected

Reverend Joseph Fain McDaniel founded **The Media Butler** to bridge the gap between creative expression and digital infrastructure. Through strategic design, trust-based systems, and advanced marketing, Joseph continues to help entrepreneurs, ministries, and innovators thrive with purpose.

Want to learn how to legally discharge any debt using a $1 postal money order? My new book explains exactly how it works, with step-by-step instructions anyone can follow.

To learn more, explore services, or connect directly with Joseph, visit:

- 🔗 JosephFainMcDaniel.com
- 🎬 IMDb Profile (https://www.imdb.com/name/nm17218641/?ref_=ext_shr_lnk)
- 🌐 The Media Butler (https://themediabutler.com/joseph-fain-mcdaniel/)
- 💼 LinkedIn (https://www.linkedin.com/in/joefmcdaniel/)

Join our private members community at:

- Title8.org

This is only the beginning.

Smart Crypto is the first of many works that empower you to step confidently into your own lane — lawfully, intelligently, and with intention.

Until next time — build wisely, live fully, and remember:

You are your own asset. Protect it accordingly.

— REVEREND JOSEPH FAIN MCDANIEL

www.ingramcontent.com/pod-product-compliance
Lightning Source LLC
LaVergne TN
LVHW022030200926
848481LV00007B/2633
* 9 7 9 8 3 3 0 2 3 7 2 8 9 *